D0359355

NARWHAL'S OTTER HALF?

ONE DAY WHEN NARWHAL AND JELLY WERE OUT FOR A SWIM ...

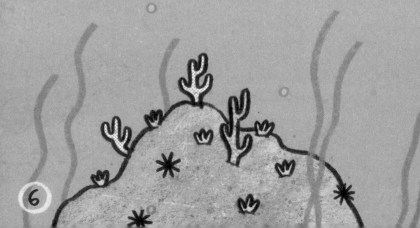

NARWHAL'S
OTTER FRIEND

BEN CLANTON

SCHOLASTIC INC.

TO THE OTTERLY AWESOME
TARA WALKER!

No part of this publication may be reproduced, stored in a retrieval system,
or transmitted in any form or by any means, electronic, mechanical, photocopying, recording,
or otherwise, without written permission of the publisher. For information regarding permission,
write to Permissions Department, Penguin Random House Canada Limited, 320 Front Street, Suite 1400,
Toronto, Ontario, Canada M5V 3B6, or email: rightscanada@penguinrandomhouse.com.

ISBN 978-1-338-65447-9

Text and illustrations copyright © 2019 by Ben Clanton.
All rights reserved. Published by Scholastic Inc., 557 Broadway, New York, NY 10012,
by arrangement with Tundra Books, a division of Penguin Random House Canada Limited.
SCHOLASTIC and associated logos are trademarks and/or registered trademarks of Scholastic Inc.

The publisher does not have any control over and does not assume any responsibility
for author or third-party websites or their content.

12 11 10 9 8 7 6 5 4 3 2   20 21 22 23 24 25

Printed in the U.S.A.   40

First Scholastic printing, January 2020

Edited by Tara Walker and Jessica Burgess
Designed by Ben Clanton

The artwork in this book was rendered in colored pencil, watercolor and ink, and colored digitally.
The text was set in a typeface based on hand lettering by Ben Clanton.

(map) © NYPL Digital Collections; (ice caps) © Maksimilian/Shutterstock; (large wave) © EpicStockMedia/Shutterstock;
(small wave) © EpicStockMedia/Shutterstock; (waffle) © Tiger Images/Shutterstock;
(strawberry) ©Valentina Razumova/Shutterstock; (pickle) © dominitsky/Shutterstock;
(spoon) © Paul Burton/Thinkstock; (pot) © Devonyu/Thinkstock; (Earth [modified]) © NASA/NOAA GOES Project;
(boom box) © valio84sl/Thinkstock; (brick) Stason4ic/Thinkstock

Species population and status information obtained from The IUCN Red List of Threatened Species as of time of printing.

CONTENTS

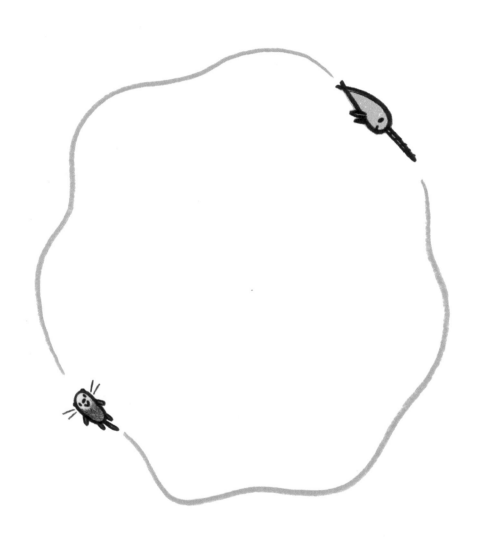

. . . AN **EXPLORER!**

THAT IS OTTERLY AWESOME!

YOU ARE AN EXPLORER?

YES SIREE!
I WANDER THE WATERS SEEKING FUN AND FINDING FRIENDS. JUST LIKE THE INCREDIBLE CAPTAIN SALLY GOODHART!

CAPTAIN GOODHART ALSO HAS OODLES OF MARVELOUS MOTTOES!

SUCH AS "SEAS THE DAY!"

"GO WITH THE FLOW!"

AND "AHOY, ADVENTURE!"

I THINK "WAFFLES! WAFFLES! WAFFLES!" WOULD MAKE A GREAT MOTTO!

CATCHY! I LIKE IT!

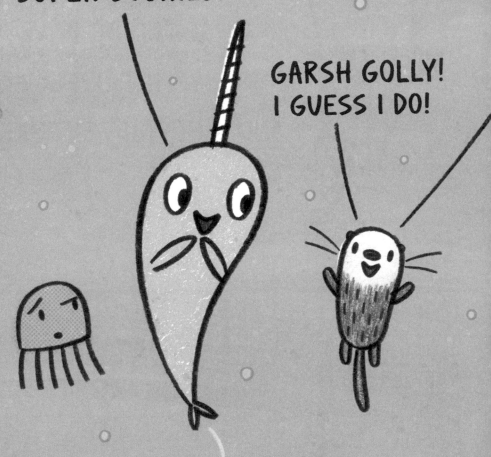

I'VE PARTIED WITH PENGUINS...

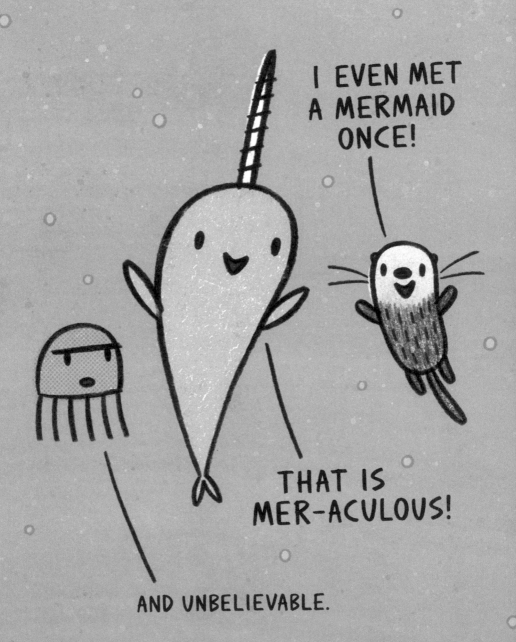

AND ONE TIME I PARTIED WITH PENGUINS WHILE SURFING WITH SEALS AND THE MERMAID I MET!

Wheee!

DUDE!

HUMPH.

YOU'VE REALLY DONE ALL THOSE THINGS?

YEPPITY YEP!

WOW!
IT SURE WOULD BE EXTRAORDINARY TO BE AN EXPLORER! ESPECIALLY WITH A FRIEND!

OH! THOSE ARE ALL GOOD THINGS TOO!

BUT THERE'S SOMETHING EVEN MORE IMPORTANT.

WAFFLESSSS!!!

OTTERLY
AWW-SOME FACTS

REAL FACTS ABOUT A REALLY ADORABLE CREATURE

THERE ARE 13 KINDS (SPECIES) OF OTTER IN THE WORLD.*

WE'RE ALL KINDS OF AWESOME!

OTTERS LIVE ON EVERY CONTINENT EXCEPT FOR AUSTRALIA AND ANTARCTICA. THEY ARE USUALLY FOUND IN OR NEAR WATER.

WHAT A WATERFUL WORLD!

*12 OF THE 13 SPECIES ARE LISTED AS THREATENED, VULNERABLE OR ENDANGERED.

OTTER FACTS

WHEEE!

OTTERS CAN BE VERY PLAYFUL AND ARE KNOWN TO ENJOY SLIDES.

ZZZ ZZZ

WHEN IN THE WATER A GROUP OF SEA OTTERS IS CALLED A RAFT. SOMETIMES RAFTING SEA OTTERS HOLD PAWS TO STAY TOGETHER WHEN SLEEPING.*

SEA OTTERS EACH HAVE A "FAVORITE" ROCK THEY KEEP IN A FOLD OF SKIN UNDER A FORELEG. THEY USE THE ROCK TO SMASH OPEN CLAMS AND SHELLFISH TO EAT.

MY PRECIOUS!

*HOWEVER, THIS IS QUITE RARE. MORE COMMONLY, OTTERS WRAP THEMSELVES IN KELP TO AVOID DRIFTING AWAY WHILE SLEEPIN

FUR-THER FACTS

BUBBLES!

SEA OTTERS USE BUBBLES TO STAY WARM! THEY TRAP BUBBLES IN THEIR FUR CREATING A "BLANKET" OF AIR THAT HELPS TO INSULATE THEM.

FUR SURE!

CALIFORNIA SEA OTTERS HAVE THE DENSEST FUR OF ANY MAMMAL ON THE PLANET: UP TO ABOUT A MILLION HAIRS PER 6.5cm^2 ($\sim 1 \text{ in.}^2$).

SOME ~~OTTER~~ FACTS
JELLYFISH

NOT BAD!

PEANUT BUTTER AND JELLYFISH? AQUARISTS (PEOPLE WHO KEEP OR MAINTAIN AQUARIUMS) AT THE CHILDREN'S AQUARIUM AT FAIR PARK IN DALLAS, TEXAS, TRIED FEEDING PEANUT BUTTER TO MOON JELLYFISH AND FOUND THAT THE JELLYFISH COULD THRIVE ON IT.

A JELLYFISH'S BODY IS MADE UP OF ABOUT 95% WATER!

WHAT-ER?!

SOME JELLYFISH CAN GLOW IN THE DARK!

HUMPH! IF NARWHAL HAS FOUND A NEW FRIEND, THEN SO WILL I.

TURTLE!
WANT TO GO EAT
WAFFLES WITH ME?

I TURTLEY WOULD!

BUT...

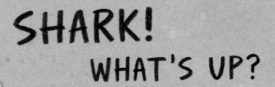

SHARK!
WHAT'S UP?

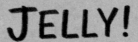

JELLY!
I'M OFF TO PLAY BUOY BALL
WITH MY BEST BUD, OCTOPUS!

HI, MR. BLOWFISH—

SORRY, JELLY!
CAN'T TALK NOW.
I'M ON THE SHELL
PHONE WITH MY
CHUM, MS. FISHY.

WHAT WAS THAT
YOU SAID, MS. FISHY?

39

THAT'S IT!

ROCKY, I THINK
YOU'RE GOING
TO BE ONE ROCK-
SOLID FRIEND.

STRAWBERRY SIDEKICK

VS.

THE dEVILed EGG

by Jelly and Rocky

SUPER WAFFLE AND STRAWBERRY SIDEKICK ARE THE GREATEST DUO EVER! NO ONE CAN STAND IN THEIR WAY!

THAT IS, UNTIL WAFFLE MEETS EGG. SUDDENLY THINGS AREN'T SO SUPER FOR STRAWBERRY.

YOU CRACK ME UP, EGG!

WAHAHA!

POOR STRAWBERRY IS COMPLETELY EGG-NORED.

AND THERE IS SOMETHING ROTTEN ABOUT THAT EGG...

CLOSE YOUR EYES, WAFFLE! I HAVE AN EGG-CELLENT SURPRISE FOR YOU. THIS WAY!

PLOP!

EGG TRIES TO SCRAMBLE OUT, BUT IT'S TOO HARD...

YOU SAVED ME!

YOU'RE NOT ONLY MY BERRY BEST BUD, YOU'RE MY HERO!

EGG'S PLANS HAVE BEEN BOILED! ER... FOILED!

AHOY, JELLY!

OH...HI,
NARWHAL...

WE'VE BEEN LOOKING ALL OVER THE WATERS FOR YOU! WHERE DID YOU GO? WHAT'S UP?

I'VE BEEN HAVING A FUNTASTIC TIME WITH MY NEW FRIEND, ROCKY.

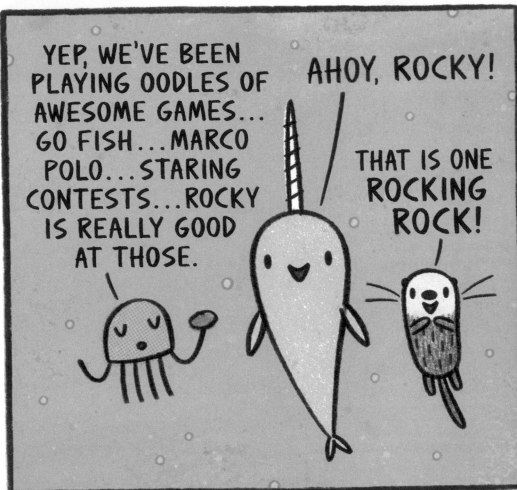

YEP, WE'VE BEEN PLAYING OODLES OF AWESOME GAMES... GO FISH...MARCO POLO...STARING CONTESTS...ROCKY IS REALLY GOOD AT THOSE.

AHOY, ROCKY!

THAT IS ONE ROCKING ROCK!

WHAT HAVE YOU BEEN UP TO?

WE'VE BEEN PLANNING...

THE AWESOMEST ADVENTURE EVER!

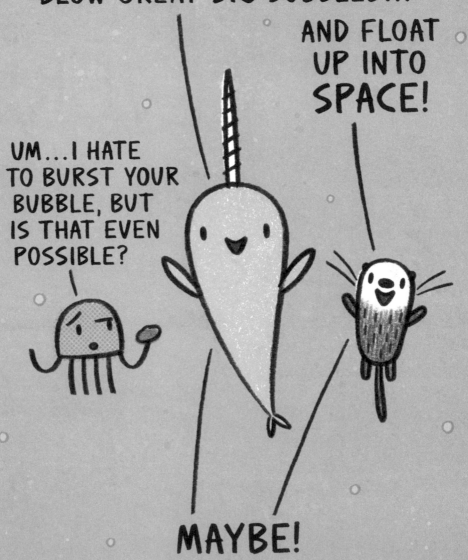

PARTY!

PARTY!

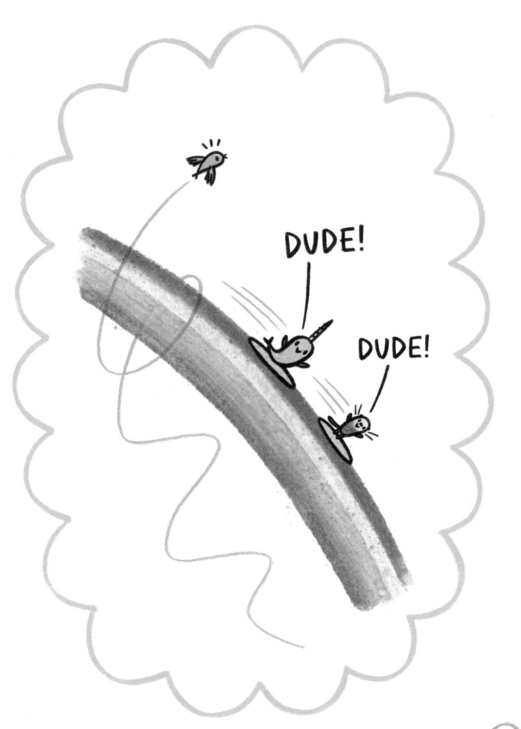

WE'RE NOT SURE WHAT COMES AFTER THE RAINBOW.

PROBABLY WAFFLES!

THAT DOES SOUND LIKE AN AMAZING ADVENTURE.

YEP! BUT SOMETHING IS STILL MISSING.

WHAT'S THAT?

ONE OF THE MOST IMPORTANT PARTS.